Martin Sherman

MESSIAH

for Joseph T. Sherman

All rights whatsoever in this play
are strictly reserved and application
for performance, etc., should be made
before rehearsal to:
Margaret Ramsay Ltd.
14a Goodwin's Court
St Martin's Lane
London WC2

No performance may be given unless a
licence has been obtained.

First published in 1982 by
Amber Lane Press Ltd.
9 Middle Way, Oxford OX2 7LH

Printed in Great Britain by
Cotswold Press Ltd., Oxford

Copyright © Martin Sherman, 1982

ISBN 0 906399 40 8

Characters

RACHEL
REBECCA
TANTA ROSE
REB ELLIS
ASHER
SARAH
Neighbours, hawkers, musicians,
SARAH's companions, etc.

The play is set in 1665, in
Yultishk, a small village on what
was once the Ukrainian border of
Poland.

NOTE
The word 'blackout' is often used
in the stage directions. It need not
be taken literally. It is meant to
suggest the end of a scene and
some change in lighting.

Messiah was first performed at Hampstead Theatre, London, on 9th December 1982. The cast included (in alphabetical order):

MATYELOK GIBBS	(Rebecca)
KEITH GILBEY	
JACK KLAFF	(Asher)
MAUREEN LIPMAN	(Rachel)
PATRICIA MARKS	(Tanta Rose)
PAULINE SIDDLE	
DESMOND STOKES	
CLIVE SWIFT	(Reb Ellis)
SHIRIN TAYLOR	(Sarah)

RONALD EYRE	(Director)
YOLANDE SONNABEND	(Settings and Costumes)
MICK HUGHES	(Lighting)
ILONA SEKACZ	(Music/Sound Designer)

Certain changes to the text may have been made during rehearsal and after this edition went to press.

[ASHER *brings a bag out from under the table.* REB ELLIS *opens the bag and brings out plums. He hands one to* RACHEL.]

Try these. It's not plum season, but you wouldn't know it, they're so juicy. Rich. A good plum flavour is rich. [*He devours a plum.*] You keep a very clean house. The Bible says it's good to be clean. Something like that, somewhere. I forget. It says a little of everything, you know, the Bible. My nephew is going to argue. He studies the Bible all day. And Talmud. And Kabbalah. Mostly, Kabbalah, eh, Asher? Demons and dybbuks in his dreams. I don't dream of demons. I dream of fruit. Plums and apples and apricots — that's why I have the finest fruit store this side of Kiev. I'm like an artist with fruit. It's not just money to me. It's love. [*He finishes his wine glass.*] This is very nice wine. Good grapes. [*He turns to* REBECCA.] Here, Rebecca, have a glass. Give your mother a glass. No, I will.

[REB ELLIS *pours another glass of wine, rises from the table and brings the glass to* REBECCA.]

You don't remember me. Reb Ellis, the fruit man? [*He turns back to* RACHEL.] I remember your mother . . . when she came back to Yultishk. We all scattered when the Cossacks came. So many were killed. But we came back. Where else to go? And one day, Rebecca returned too. So beautiful, so sad. Like a pomegranate. Holding your hand. You were a little girl, you don't remember. Four years wandering around Poland. Ach, what she must have seen. No wonder she doesn't talk. I don't think she's ill. [*He turns back to* REBECCA.] You just don't have anything more to say, do you?

[*He tries to put the glass in her hand, but she will not let go of her wool.*]

Drink. It's good.

[*Frustrated, he puts the drink down by her chair. He kneels and takes out a plum.*]

Well, how about a plum? I'll leave the plum — right here — for you — if you decide later, on your own, to have it.

[*He puts the plum in her lap, then rises and walks back to the table.*]

Your mother has beautiful eyes. Green. Greengage eyes. You don't talk much, do you? I like a quiet woman. Keeps a clean house. My nephew, Asher, I brought him because I thought he could speak for me. I get very shy. But at the same time, I can get along anywhere. I'm like that. Peasants or kings. I fit in. My nephew, Asher, keeps looking for the Messiah. In the Kabbalah, he looks, in the Kabbalah. He says the time is coming, the time is coming. I tell you something, if the Messiah comes tomorrow, it's not Asher who could talk to him. Asher can talk to books. *I'd* talk to him. We'd sit down and have a peach. Or a pear. Although if he comes tomorrow it wouldn't be a pear. The crop's not so good this year. I wouldn't give the Messiah a bad pear, believe me. Only the best. And we'd get along. [*He pours another glass of wine.*] I know human nature. That's in the Bible, too. Somewhere. So, you see, I'm quiet. I'm shy. But I get along. Peasants or kings. Messiahs. You name it. I get along. So I'm not a bad person to marry. There. That's what I want to say. You'll make a nice dinner table for me. You'll keep a clean house for me. You'll be happy. [*He rises.*] All right, Asher, you did a good job. Give her the oranges. You didn't give her the oranges.

[*Blackout.*]

Lights rise on RACHEL *praying.*

RACHEL: God help me. Look, we're going to have to sort this

out. What an exasperating man. He talks and talks and talks . . . But I don't dislike him. He spoke to Mama. You've seen for years what's happened here. People come in. They never speak to Mama. She's crazy. She's cursed. She's dead. To this whole goddamned town, she's dead. I'm sorry. I didn't mean to take your name in vain. I'm sorry. I'm sorry. Forgive me. Oh God . . . [*Pause.*] You see, the thing is that he's ugly. And I'm not sure that I care what's underneath. Now his nephew . . . His nephew is beautiful. For all I know he's an absolute idiot, but *outside*, the part with bones and tissue and flesh, *that* part — beautiful. *Him* I would marry. Oh but God, it doesn't make sense, me of all people. When all I want — all I live for — is for someone to look beneath *my* face and see that *I'm* beautiful. Underneath the spots. Can't you take away the spots? Oh, forget it, I didn't mean to ask you again. And the teeth. I know you don't want to discuss the teeth. It's just that sometimes I forget about them. And then I pass a mirror . . . It's like lightning struck my mouth and then stayed there. The teeth! I sit here all day and try to think of some use for them. And what do I come up with? If I'm ever attacked by a lion, I can bite back. There are no lions in Yultishk. You know, if I wrote the Ten Commandments on them — five on one, five on the other — there certainly is room — and then walked out on the street, I could say *I* was the Messiah. I think and think . . . there must be a reason for them. You have reasons for everything. Don't you? [*Pause.*] So. I'm ugly. That's that. So. Who better than me to forget about Reb Ellis' fat and Reb Ellis' smell, and see the bright, blue-eyed Reb Ellis inside? But I *can't*. I can't even look at an ugly man. If the Messiah came today, and he had warts and a big belly, I would send him back. Oh God. Help me. Give me a sign.

A sign. Something. A rainbow. Thunder. Locusts. Something. Do I marry him? Talk to me. Burn me a bush and talk to me. Do I marry him? [*Silence.*] He spoke to Mama. No one else has.

[*Blackout.*]

A Hebraic melody pierces the darkness. Lights rise slowly. RACHEL is standing in a wedding dress. She looks awkward and embarrassed. TANTA ROSE and REBECCA are with her.

TANTA ROSE: Rachela, you're a beautiful bride.

[RACHEL *winces.*]

What? You make faces. If only your father were here to see you. May his soul rest.in peace.

[REBECCA *looks away.*]

Rebecca, tell her. Tell her she's a beautiful bride.

[REBECCA *wanders away from them.*]

RACHEL: Tanta. Just let it be.

[RACHEL *and* TANTA *go after* REBECCA.]

A table sits in the centre of the field. REB ELLIS is at the head of the table. RACHEL is at one side, with REBECCA and TANTA ROSE. An old RABBI is on the other side. They all have wine. REB ELLIS is making a toast.

REB ELLIS: A toast! To my handsome bride.

[RACHEL *smiles at the word 'handsome'.*]

To my friends. My family, such as it is. They're all dead, killed by the Cossacks. They can't see this happy day. There's only my nephew Asher left, and where is he? Disappeared! Ach! He's young. He's probably studying the Kabbalah somewhere. He forgot what day it was. I'll have a new family. To my new family. [*He pours another glass.*] To Rebecca, my new mother-in-law. What every man wants, a quiet mother-in-law.

[*He drinks.* RACHEL, *despite herself, laughs. She looks at*
REB ELLIS *with a certain affection.*]

So. [*He pours another drink.*] To the town. To the orchards.
The fields. The trees that bear my beautiful fruit. To the
apples, the prunes, the pears . . .

[ASHER *runs in. He is in a state of ecstasy. He has letters
in his hand.*]

ASHER: Uncle! He's here.

REB ELLIS: Asher. A toast. I'm making a toast.

ASHER: He's here!

REB ELLIS: Asher. Take a seat. It's my wedding day. [*To the
guests.*] He forgets. He reads too much.

ASHER: *He's here!*

[RACHEL *rises.*]

RACHEL: *Who's* here?

[TANTA ROSE *pulls* RACHEL *down.*]

TANTA ROSE: Shh! Rachel!

ASHER: The Messiah! The Messiah is here!

REB ELLIS: Asher. Not on my wedding day. I was making a
toast . . .

ASHER: Uncle, it's true. The Messiah is here. Look. Letters. I
have letters. Reb Samuel, the merchant in Kiev, received
them. He made copies. His messenger brought them this
afternoon. I've read them and read them. Here. See.
Letters. [*He opens a letter.*] This one. From Nathan of
Gaza. A holy man. [*He reads from the letter.*] "Hear me, my
brothers, for our Messiah has come. He was born in
Izmir. His name is Sabbatai Sevi." [*He throws the letter
onto the table.*] Nathan is a famous rabbi, Uncle. He
doesn't make things up. Look. Letters. They tell the
story of Sabbatai Sevi. Here. [*He throws another letter on the
table.*] Ordained a rabbi at eighteen. Speaks aloud the
sacred and forbidden name of God at twenty. In
Salonica, he takes a Torah scroll as his bride. In a

wedding ceremony. He *marries* the Torah! Think of that, Uncle! This *must* be the Messiah. In Jerusalem, he performs miracles and raises part of the temple. And now in Gaza, Nathan, the holy man, recognizes him as the Messiah — and he himself, Sabbatai himself, always silent on this subject, finally declares himself. I *am* the Messiah, he says. I *am* the Messiah! Look. Letters. Proof. [*He throws the other letters on the table.*] He leaves for Izmir again and eventually Constantinople where he's going to take the crown from the Sultan's head. And look, Uncle, news . . . [*He takes out another letter.*] News of the tribes. The ten lost tribes of Israel. They've been found. Someone saw them in Arabia, by the river Sambatyon, ready to march, ready to cross the river, ready to take vengeance on our enemies. And Uncle, the teachings always said the Messiah would come after a great catastrophe. And didn't we have a great catastrophe seventeen years ago? Right here in Poland. Our people massacred . . . What for? What *for*? To prepare for the Messiah! And now he's come. He's come in the name of our Lord. He's come as our king. And we can all leave Yultishk, we can all leave Poland, and go back, back to Jerusalem! But first — we must purge ourselves. Repent our sins. Destroy our guilt. So we can be pure in his presence. Uncle! The drums of heaven are beating. Uncle! Listen! Listen to them. Uncle! The Messiah is here!

    [ASHER *faints.*]

    [*Blackout.*]

Lights rise on RACHEL *praying.*

RACHEL: I wanted a quiet wedding. Dear God . . . why do you play jokes on me? No one in Yultishk will ever forget my wedding. Who is this Sabbatai? I'm so confused . . .

[*Pause.*] Do you know what it was like? Our wedding night? What a question! Of course you know. You saw it. You see everything. You're always there, aren't you, when people make love? No, promise me, promise me, that wasn't making love. Something else, that was something else, but not making love. I'm so smart, but I'm so dumb. I know so much and I know so little. But even if he wasn't fat, even if he didn't smell, even if he was lean and golden and beautiful, that would not have been making love. He hurt me. And hurt me. And then ignored me. And I know about my teeth, but if my teeth were *his* teeth, I still wouldn't have done that to *him*. Well. He's a man. So be it. He's a man. [*Pause.*] If you see everything, if you know everything already — then what's the point, what's the point in talking to you?

    [*Blackout.*]

Lights rise on the kitchen of REB ELLIS' *house. Fruit everywhere. Expensive furniture.* REBECCA *is sitting.* TANTA ROSE *is talking to* RACHEL.

TANTA ROSE: So — Reb Yitsel's sister received a letter from Reb Jacom's brother in Prague and he said that he heard that in Salonica they're marrying all their children off — ten, eleven years old — to each other, so they can start having babies right away. All I could think of was, what a job for a matchmaker.

RACHEL: Why are they doing that?

TANTA ROSE: So there won't be any more unborn souls left.

RACHEL: So?

TANTA ROSE: So as soon as that happens, the Messiah is free to accept his crown. It says so somewhere.

RACHEL: Tanta, we don't know if this man really is the Messiah.

TANTA ROSE: So then why did Asher faint?

RACHEL: He forgot to eat.

TANTA ROSE: How do you know he's *not* the Messiah? Did God tell you?

> [*Silence.*]

RACHEL: I'm not talking to God.

> [*Blackout.*]

Lights rise on REB ELLIS' *kitchen.* RACHEL *is attending to* REBECCA. ASHER *runs in through the back door.*

ASHER: Are there nettles?

RACHEL: Are there *what*?

ASHER: Nettles.

RACHEL: Where?

ASHER: In the house.

RACHEL: Of course not.

ASHER: I *need* nettles.

RACHEL: What for?

ASHER: To beat myself.

> [RACHEL *laughs.*]

Why are you laughing?

RACHEL: I'm not.

> [*She starts to laugh again.*]

ASHER: It's not funny. Sabbatai beats himself with nettles every day. And can his sins be greater than mine?

RACHEL: How old are you?

ASHER: Twenty-four.

RACHEL: And how great are your sins?

ASHER: Great! Believe me. *Great*! I have impure thoughts. [*Silence.*] You wouldn't understand. Women don't have them.

> [ASHER *rushes out through the door.* RACHEL *laughs.*]

RACHEL: Mama, Mama, Mama . . .

> [*Blackout.*]

Lights rise on REB ELLIS' *kitchen.* RACHEL *is with* REBECCA. REB
ELLIS *comes in from the next room.*

REB ELLIS: Have you seen my nephew? That boy is obsessed.
Sabbatai this, Sabbatai that . . . And it's spreading all
over town. Reb Fishel's daughter had a vision. She saw a
burning moon. I think she had a fever. She's only thir-
teen. I sent her some oranges. And speaking of oranges, I
spoke to the Rabbi. He said there's a special prayer for
orange rinds. I noticed the other day you said the prayer
for fruit over some orange rinds. I'm not criticizing. You
said it very well. I tell all my friends, you keep a wonder-
ful house, you know all the prayers; but orange rinds are
considered to be a scent not a food, so there's a special
prayer — "bore minei besamin." In the opinion of some
— but not all — you can say that prayer over lemon rinds
as well. But you know how rabbis are with opinions.
Talk, talk, talk. They could talk you to death . . .

[*He rushes back into the next room.*]

RACHEL: Oh Mama, Mama, Mama . . .

[*Blackout.*]

Lights rise on REB ELLIS' *kitchen.* RACHEL *is with* REBECCA.
ASHER *comes in through the back door.*

ASHER: I'm sorry.

RACHEL: What?

ASHER: I apologize.

RACHEL: What for?

ASHER: Saying you wouldn't understand. A letter came to
town yesterday all the way from Venice. And in it it says
that Sabbatai says that women are equal. Equal. To us.
He's removed the curse that was set upon Eve. He
dances with his wife, Sarah. He takes her to the
synagogue with him and lets her read from the Torah. So

perhaps I was wrong. Perhaps you do have impure thoughts.

RACHEL: Perhaps.

ASHER: Then you should beat yourself with nettles too. Why should it just be the men? Half of the men in town are doing it already? Why not half the women? It's a new world . . . The problem is so many people are beating themselves with nettles that there are no nettles left. We'll have to send to Kiev.

[RACHEL *laughs.*]

You're laughing again.

RACHEL: No.

[*A pause.* ASHER *takes the comb from* RACHEL*'s hand and puts it on the table.*]

ASHER: Do you believe in him?

RACHEL: Who?

ASHER: Sabbatai. Who else?

[RACHEL *is silent.*]

Sabbatai says we have to ask women their opinions.

RACHEL: Oh. [*Silence.*] Well. I like what he says about women. *If* he says it. They're all rumours. Stories. Don't you think we need a sign from God? [*Pause.*] I don't know. That's my answer. I don't know.

ASHER: Look.

[*He takes off his shirt, and turns around, showing her his back, which is marked and bruised and discoloured.*]

For four nights I've been purging myself. Because I *do* know. I don't need a sign.

[*He turns back.* RACHEL *is silent. She stares at his body, which is lithe and handsome.*]

I've waited and waited. I've pored over the Kabbalah. I have no family. Only Uncle. My parents were murdered by the Cossacks. I've always known the Messiah would come. For the sake of my parents. Why do you look at me

that way? Do you think I'm mad? [*Silence.*] We're supposed
to ask women what they're thinking. [*Silence.*] What are
you thinking?

> [RACHEL *takes the comb from the table and starts to comb*
> REBECCA's *hair.*]

RACHEL: I can't tell you what I'm thinking.

> [*Blackout.*]

Lights rise on RACHEL *praying.*

RACHEL: Blessed God, we have to talk. I was angry at you, I
wasn't going to speak to you ever again, but we *have to
talk*! I've never seen a man's body before. Reb Ellis never
undresses in front of me. And when he comes into bed, it
must always be dark. Well, those are *your* laws. Or at
least laws made in your name — some day we have to
discuss that. But with Reb Ellis, believe me, your laws
are fine. You must have made them because you knew so
many women marry fat, ugly men. But suppose a
woman marries an Asher? Then what an awful law! Oh
Lord, do you realize a man's chest can be beautiful, not
just his face? And perhaps a woman's chest too . . . To a
man. My breasts . . . Did you ever think about that? My
breasts may be very nice. So if that's the case why can't I
wear clothes around my face and leave my breasts bare?
[*Pause.*] I'm having impure thoughts. Oh, am I having
impure thoughts. He asked me what I was thinking.
How could I tell him? He'd run out and find me a nettle.
But he is so beautiful that now I want to believe in his
Messiah. And that's not right. One thing shouldn't mix
itself up with the other. Why do you make everything so
confusing? [*Pause.*] I'm sorry. Forgive me for the things I
say. I love you. You saved me from the Cossacks. You do
care. I know that. You're just quiet. Like Mama. [*Pause.*]

I haven't really seen a man's body. Only *half* a man's body. [*Silence.*] Only half.
> [*Blackout.*]

Lights rise on REB ELLIS' *kitchen.* REB ELLIS *and* RACHEL *are at the table.* REB ELLIS *is drinking a glass of tea. The teapot is on the table.* RACHEL *is sewing.* REBECCA *is sitting at the side.*

REB ELLIS: It's good tea.

RACHEL: Thank you.

REB ELLIS: You make good tea.

RACHEL: Thank you.

REB ELLIS: Have you seen my nephew? I hate to go outside and look for him. It's so cold outside. I've never liked the cold. I'm afraid I'll find him buried in the snow. Reb Ginsel buried himself in the snow last week for three days. And then he went home and sold his business. And now he sits waiting for the call to Jerusalem. He'll never get to Jerusalem. He'll die from bad lungs. From burying himself in the snow. Of course it's better than hot wax. Reb Lerner poured hot wax over his body. Then he sold *his* business. Every day there's a new report, a new rumour, a new letter. Sabbatai is in Izmir. Everyone's tense. Everyone's expecting something. The day of redemption is coming. Asher says that. The day of redemption. I'm cold. It gets cold inside. Is there more tea?

> [RACHEL *pours him another cup of tea.*]

You make good tea.

RACHEL: Thank you.

REB ELLIS: You're a quiet woman. I like a quiet woman. I can talk to you. I love tea when it burns my mouth. That's how I'll purge myself, eh? Drinking hot tea. [*Pause.*] What happens if my nephew is right? What happens if

Reb Ginsel and Reb Lemer know what they're doing?
What happens if Sabbatai goes to Constantinople and is
crowned by the Sultan, and says, at last: my people, my
people, your suffering is over, the day of redemption is
here. What happens? A little more. Hot tea.

[RACHEL *pours him another cup.*]

Thank you. You know when the Cossacks came . . . It's
good tea. Good tea.

RACHEL: Thank you.

REB ELLIS: I hid in my fruit store. When the Cossacks came. I
ran away from my family. My parents were old. Still. I
ran away. It didn't make any sense. The Cossacks came
everywhere. But I felt safe there. In my fruit store. Well,
eventually they arrived. They broke down the door and
marched in. I was in a corner, hunched over, in a corner.
And then — I don't know what possessed me — I got up
and walked to their captain and took a nectarine from a
basket. A fresh, beautiful nectarine. And I handed it to
him. He took it. He bit into it. It was good. And he
walked out. And his men followed him. They didn't
touch me. Or the store. I never understood it. [*Silence.*] I
don't keep nectarines any more. [*Silence.*] All those fools
outside. They bury themselves in snow. They pour hot
wax on their bodies. And what do they repent? Little
things. And I sit here. And I have committed the
greatest crime in all of Yultishk. Even though I don't
know what it is.

[RACHEL *goes to him and takes his hand. The gesture
startles him. He holds her hand for a moment, then
brushes it away.*]

I'd like some more tea.

[*Blackout.*]

Lights rise on RACHEL *praying.*

RACHEL: Help us, God. Please. Help us. It's getting out of hand. The whole town is going crazy. People are falling down. All day, all night. And foaming at the mouth. They're all screaming salvation is here. Everybody is seeing Elijah. In the market. In the synagogue. On the street. Sitting at the dinner table. Elijah. Well, I still haven't seen him. But I'm so confused. I want to believe our suffering is over. I want to believe in Sabbatai. But I need a sign. Reb Ellis is behaving strangely too. Yesterday he lay in the yard and had a huge stone put on his chest. Today he gave lemons away in his store. For free. Cyprus lemons! It's getting out of hand.

    [*Blackout.*]

Lights rise on REB ELLIS' *kitchen.* RACHEL *is sitting at the table, sewing.* REBECCA *is sitting in a corner.* REB ELLIS *comes in from the back door. He is in a frenzy. He bends down and examines the chair* RACHEL *is sitting in.*

REB ELLIS: This is a nice chair. I always liked this chair.

    [*He rises and takes a medallion out of his pocket.*]

I have a present for you. My cousin from Hamburg sent it to me. It has a drawing of Sabbatai. Look, he's riding on a dragon. And — look — above him — gold and precious stones falling from Heaven. The day of redemption. [*Pause.*] All the way from Hamburg. Even in Germany they're talking about Sabbatai. Here. It's for you. You're a good wife, you keep a clean house.

    [*He hands her the medallion.*]

Here.

RACHEL: Thank you.

    [*He sits down at the table next to her.*]

REB ELLIS: My nephew tells me I'm supposed to ask you ques-

tions. Opinions. Sabbatai says women have opinions.
Well, you know these Messiahs, they have some strange
ideas. But this is a *real* Messiah. What do you think? You
see, if he is real, I have to be free of everything. All my
sins. All my material possessions. There's no way I can
carry a fruit store to Jerusalem, is there? What do you
think? Well. I sold the fruit store. To some goyim in the
next town. Do you think I was right? I want your opinion.
They say Sarah, Sabbatai's wife, influences his decisions.
Reb Bisek heard rumours that she was a whore in
Amsterdam. Others say she's a saint. Ach, who's to
know? But she couldn't keep as good a house as you. I
tell all my friends that. [*He brushes the back of her chair.*]
I've always liked this chair. It's a pretty wood. So I sold
the store. And all the fruit. All the fruit! Qumquats
arrived yesterday, so beautiful; and today strawberries
— fresh, *luscious* . . . Well, you can't take strawberries to
Jerusalem. Can you? Do you think I'm right? And I sold
the house. More goyim. And I'm giving away everything. Everything I own. All my possessions. That's why
I want you to have this medallion. I want it to be yours.
Always. You're going to have to stand up. Do you think
I'm doing the right thing?

    [*He pulls her up. He feels her chair again.*]
It's a nice chair. Belonged to my mother.

    [REB ELLIS *takes her chair — and his own — and walks
    to the back door. He opens the door. He heaves the chairs
    into the yard. He walks back into the kitchen.*]
Can you help me with the table?

RACHEL: The table?

    [REB ELLIS *takes hold of the kitchen table. He motions
    *RACHEL *to the other side.*]

REB ELLIS: Take that end.

    [RACHEL *takes the other end. Together they inch towards*

[*the door, carrying the table.*]

My cousin wrote from Hamburg that Sabbatai was
changing all the feast days. He's changing *all* the laws.
All the laws. It's a new age. What do you think? Lift it
out the door. Right.

[*They push the table through the door.* REB ELLIS *gives it
a further push outside.* REB ELLIS *runs back into the room
and starts picking up utensils, vases, pictures — anything
he can lay his hands on. He runs back and forth to the
door, grabbing things and heaving them out.*]

They say Sabbatai sings psalms in a golden voice. He
sings Castilian love songs to the Torah. Well, listen, if
you're a Messiah, you can sing what you want. What do
you think of that? Sometimes he seems strange this
Sabbatai, don't you think?

RACHEL: No! Not the teapot!

[REB ELLIS *heaves the teapot out through the back door.
He picks up dishes and plates and starts throwing them
out.* RACHEL *tries to hide whatever she's fond of.*]

REB ELLIS: I could talk to him, you know. I'm sure Sabbatai
and I would get along. I would sit him down at our table
— well, no longer — we'd have to stand — and I'd say,
Sabbatai, tell me which day exactly is going to be the day
of redemption.

[*He pauses at the door. He turns and looks at* RACHEL. *He
starts to weep.*]

I'm afraid. I'm afraid he'll look into my heart. Do you
understand?

[*He goes over to* REBECCA. *He looks at* REBECCA*'s chair.
He pats her on the shoulder.*]

Sit, Rebecca. I'm sure the Bible says we can keep your
chair.

[*He walks into the next room.* ASHER *runs in through the
back door.*]

ASHER: It's a miracle. You should see the yard. He's throwing away his worldly goods. He's cleansed his soul. He sold the store. The *fruit* store. It's a miracle.

[RACHEL *grabs* ASHER*'s arm, then, quickly, withdraws her hand.*]

RACHEL: Stop him.

ASHER: What?

RACHEL: Please.

ASHER: What are you talking about?

RACHEL: Stop him.

ASHER: You don't believe in Sabbatai. He does.

[REB ELLIS *comes out of the next room carrying handfuls of clothes. He runs past them. He heaves the clothing out through the back door. He runs back into the next room.*]

RACHEL: *Stop him!*

ASHER: Can't you recognize a miracle when it happens in front of your own eyes?

[REB ELLIS *comes out of the next room carrying sheets and bedspreads. He is all tangled up in them. He throws them out through the back door. He starts back for the next room when he notices a bag on the floor. He examines it.*]

REB ELLIS: What's this? Oh, I forgot. I was going to give you these grapefruit. Well. For the poor, eh?

[*He takes a grapefruit out of the bag and examines it lovingly.*]

Such beautiful grapefruit. Perhaps if we kept a few. Look how ripe they are. Just this one. For dinner.

[*He puts the grapefruit back into the bag.*]

No. No.

[*He heaves the bag of grapefruit out through the back door.*]

My soul is clean. Now my soul is clean. I've given away my life. I'll start a new one in Jerusalem. Why doesn't he tell us what day it will be? My soul is spotless. It can

climb the sky. It can sit with Sabbatai in Heaven. You
know, the Bible says, when the Messiah comes, man will
soar up to the clouds. Says it somewhere. To the clouds.
Think of that! If Sabbatai looks into my heart and sees
that it's pure, he'll let me soar into the clouds.

ASHER: He's possessed. A holy spirit has entered his soul. His
heart is pure now. He knows things. Things we don't
know. He's in a state of grace. If he says he can fly to
Jerusalem, then he can. All he ever cared about was
money and fruit. And he gave it all away. That's one
miracle. So why can't there be two?

RACHEL: The day of Redemption isn't here yet. Stop him!

REB ELLIS: When the Messiah comes, the angels will carry us
to Jerusalem on their wings. It says so in the Bible.
Somewhere. We can fly to Jerusalem.

   [*He goes into the next room.*]

ASHER: I'm not sure that *is* in the Bible.

RACHEL: Then tell him that.

   [REB ELLIS *comes out of the next room, carrying a ladder.*]

REB ELLIS: If my heart is pure, I can soar . . .

   [*He goes out through the back door with the ladder.*]
   [*Blackout.*]

The lights rise on REB ELLIS' *back yard. The yard is cluttered with
half the contents of* REB ELLIS' *house. The wall of his house leads
to a roof.* REB ELLIS *puts the ladder against the wall and starts to
climb.* RACHEL *and* ASHER *run into the yard.*

RACHEL: Where's he going?

ASHER: Uncle! Where are you going?

REB ELLIS: [*climbing*] To Heaven.

RACHEL: Make him come down.

   [TANTA ROSE *arrives. She looks up at* REB ELLIS. REB
   ELLIS *reaches the roof. He pulls the ladder up with him.
   He stands on the roof.*]

REB ELLIS: I can fly. I can fly to Jerusalem. I will be there to greet the Messiah. He will arrive on a dragon. He will wear a white prayer shawl. He will carry a silver fan, and touch the people on the street with it. He will call out the sacred, forbidden name of God. And Elijah will ride beside him. I'll be able to see it for myself. I can fly!

[*Two* NEIGHBOURS *arrive.*]

TANTA ROSE: Reb Ellis! What are you doing?

1ST NEIGHBOUR: Come down.

[REB ELLIS *looks at the sky; he hesitates.*]

REB ELLIS: I know I can fly. But I'm afraid. If I'm afraid, something is wrong. My heart isn't pure. My soul isn't saved.

[*A* VAGRANT *has arrived and is picking through the objects on the ground, carting some of them off.*]

1ST NEIGHBOUR: Reb Ellis!

2ND NEIGHBOUR: Come down!

[REB ELLIS *points to something on the ground.*]

REB ELLIS: Look. Look! The grapefruit are still in the box. Asher, give out the grapefruit. And then I can fly.

[ASHER *hesitates, then goes to the box of grapefruit, and starts handing them out.* RACHEL *runs back into the kitchen.* RACHEL *prays.*]

RACHEL: Dear God in Heaven, stop him! Don't let him jump. He'll break his neck. The Bible says nothing about flying to Jerusalem. They've all gone mad. He's not a bad man, you know. All right, he talks too much; all right, he doesn't listen; all right, when the lights are off, he's not so gentle. But, still, in his way, he's kind. Don't let him jump. Make it rain. If it's wet, he'll come down. He won't want to catch cold. Make him come to his senses. This whole town will do anything, anything, in the name of the Messiah. But what kind of Messiah would let that man jump? Look, who wants the Messiah more than I do? Every day since I could speak, I've prayed for him to come. And if Sabbatai is the Messiah, I'll rejoice . . . But there has to be some kind of proof. Not rumours. Not letters from Hamburg. Not pretty medallions. *Proof.* I know how reluctant you are to give signs, but if ever we needed one . . . From *you*. Something. Something we all can see. Not some little girl waking up in the middle of the night and saying the moon is on fire. Something we *all* can see. A special rainbow. A ladder from the sky. A dead man rising. A dead man flying. [*Pause.*] A live man flying. [*Pause.*] Oh, my God. [*Pause.*] No. No, this must be in my mind. This can't be you. You're not talking to me, are you? You're not talking to me at last? [*Pause.*] A man flying. Can I be that blind? Is this your sign? [*Pause.*] No, I'm going mad too. Like everyone else. [*Pause.*] Asher said if a miracle happens in front of my eyes, I would not see it. Have I been staring you in the face? At last? And not recognizing you? If a man can fly . . . [*Pause.*] No. Not Reb Ellis. Reb Ellis can't fly. Reb Ellis can't be a sign. [*Pause.*] Can he? [*Pause.*] Then is he here? Is the Messiah really here? Did the moon really catch fire? Are you really going to save us? Do we never have to worry about the Cossacks again? Do I never have to think about my teeth again? Is it a new world? Can it be happening? Have all my prayers come true? If a man can fly . . . [*Pause.*] *This* man? Not this man. [*Pause.*] Why do I doubt you? Oh dear God! Why do I *doubt* you? Forgive me. I'm not worthy of you. Thank you. Thank you. Let the man fly. Let *this* man fly. Let the clouds open. Let the angels carry him to Jerusalem. Let him fly!

> [RACHEL *walks out of the back door and into the yard.*
> *She looks up to the roof.*]

Reb Ellis!

[REB ELLIS *looks down at her.*]

Jump!

[*Blackout.*]

Lights rise on RACHEL *praying.*

RACHEL: God bless Mama. God bless Tanta Rose. God bless
Asher. God bless the soul of poor Reb Ellis. [*Pause.*] It's
not your fault. [*Pause.*] What can I say? I wanted a sign.
[*Blackout.*]

Lights rise on REB ELLIS' *kitchen.* REBECCA *is sitting in the
corner, in the only chair. Objects are scattered on the floor. The
medallion of Sabbatai lies on the floor.* RACHEL *and* ASHER *are
standing. They are very awkward with each other.*

ASHER: Well . . .

[*Silence.*]

RACHEL: Well . . .

[*Silence.*]

ASHER: Well . . .

[*Silence.*]

RACHEL: I'm sorry I can't give you tea.

ASHER: He gave away the teapot.

RACHEL: Yes.

[*Silence.*]

ASHER: Well . . .

[*Silence.*]

RACHEL: It was *my* teapot.

ASHER: Oh. [*Pause.*] I don't know if he's allowed to give away
your worldly goods. Are yours his? It's a fine point. Ask
the Rabbi. Uncle never really knew the laws. Or the
Bible. He imagined things. He made them up. But with
something like the Messiah, of course, you can't make
things up. [*Pause.*] He wasn't ready. For Jerusalem.

[*Pause.*] Why don't you come with me?

RACHEL: Come with you?

ASHER: To Constantinople.

[RACHEL *blushes and turns away.*]

We're a family.

RACHEL: I have to sit shiva.

ASHER: You can't. He threw out the wooden benches.

RACHEL: I'll borrow.

ASHER: You have no place to live.

RACHEL: I'll find some place.

ASHER: You have nothing to do.

RACHEL: I'll sew.

ASHER: If we go to Odessa, there are boats.

RACHEL: Boats. I've never seen a boat.

ASHER: If the owners are Jewish, they'll take us for free. Holy
pilgrims. In Constantinople, he will unseat the Sultan.
And he'll be crowned king of the Jews. We can be there,
and then we can follow him to Jerusalem.

RACHEL: Don't you ever doubt?

ASHER: No.

RACHEL: Never?

ASHER: Never.

RACHEL: Not even when Reb Ellis came crashing down?

ASHER: He wasn't ready.

RACHEL: I thought it would be a sign. I prayed to God for a
sign. That Sabbatai was really the Messiah.

ASHER: I don't need a sign.

RACHEL: I do.

ASHER: Why does God have to give a sign just for you?

[RACHEL *turns away.*]

ASHER: I'm going.

[RACHEL *doesn't look at him.*]

I'll send you letters.

RACHEL: Letters. More letters about the Messiah.

ASHER: You can change your mind.
> [*Pause.*]

RACHEL: I've never seen a boat.
> [*She smiles.*]

ASHER: Then come with me, Tanta.

RACHEL: Tanta?
> [*She looks at him in horror.*]

ASHER: We're a family. Uncle would want us to stay together.

RACHEL: [*Looks up, towards God.*] Tanta!

ASHER: You're the only family I have.

RACHEL: I have Mama. And God.

ASHER: They're both silent.

RACHEL: I need a sign.

ASHER: You're stubborn.

RACHEL: One day everything was quiet. Yultishk was like a river. Nothing — except the Cossacks — could disturb it. The next day, I'm married, and you're fainting and the whole town is going crazy, because somebody we never heard of sent some letters. We don't even know if there *is* a Sabbatai. And if there is, and if he is the Messiah, God will tell us in some way. And not by pushing Reb Ellis off the roof. [*Pause.*] I'll tell you something terrible. I don't think it had anything to do with Sabbatai. I think I really just wanted him to jump. [*Pause.*] No. If Sabbatai is the Messiah, God will find his own way to let us know. [*Pause.*] There. That's what you wanted. A woman's thoughts.
> [*Silence.*]

ASHER: I'm going.

RACHEL: Go. Send me letters.

ASHER: Yes.
> [*Silence. He goes to the door.*]
> Goodbye.
> [*He leaves.* RACHEL *watches him.* REBECCA *rises and*

> *walks to the centre of the room. She sits on the floor and*
> *picks up the medallion.*]

REBECCA: [*Whispers.*] Sabbatai. [*She rises and holds the medallion.*]
Sabbatai.

> [RACHEL *turns and looks at her.*]

RACHEL: Mama!

REBECCA: Sabbatai!

RACHEL: Dear God.

REBECCA: Sabbatai! Sabbatai!

> [RACHEL *calls out the door.*]

RACHEL: Asher! Come back! He's sent a sign!

REBECCA: Sabbatai! Sabbatai! Sabbatai!

> [RACHEL *runs and embraces* REBECCA. *She holds* REBECCA
> *in her arms.* ASHER *returns and stands in the doorway.*]

CURTAIN

Act Two

Lights rise on RACHEL *praying.*

RACHEL: Dear God, I never want to see a boat again. Up and down. Up and down. Up and down. Everyone is ill. Except Mama. Mama is calm. Yesterday I could not take the up and down anymore. I screamed, "Please God, let me die." Thank heaven — as usual — you didn't pay attention to me. We're almost there. Almost to Constantinople. But Sabbatai is some place else. He's in a castle. A fortress. A prison. There are so many stories, who knows the truth? Even on a boat, there are stories. Even on a boat, people bring out letters. Where do they find them? Floating in the sea? Well, the letters that have dried have said Sabbatai arrived in Constantinople and was arrested by the Turks and they sent him to — this castle or this fortress or this prison in a place called Gallipoli, and there he sits like a king and receives visitors, and thousands of Jews from all over the world have come to Gallipoli and the Turks are afraid to harm him because they know he's the Messiah. Dear God, after a boat trip like this, he *better* be the Messiah. Asher says I still doubt. I don't doubt. It's just that sometimes I *question*. I question everything. Except Asher's eyes. But that's a different story. It's not enough he sees my spots, it's not enough he sees my teeth, you had to make me his Tanta in the bargain. My heart goes up and down, up and down, like this boat. Life was simpler when I was just sewing, and there was no nephew, and there was no Messiah. Well. Enough of that. Your ears must burn with all our complaints. If you make the sea calm, I'd be happy. If we get to Gallipoli, I'd be happy.

No matter how unhappy I am, if I'm on land, I'd be happy.

[*Blackout.*]

A flute. A Spanish Melody.

Lights rise on an open square in Gallipoli. People. Colour. Noise. Voices coming from all directions. A VISIONARY *stands on a rock, talking in a frenzy. A young* SINGER *is humming the Spanish tune to the sound of the flute.* TURKS *are hawking wares — drawings, paintings, parchments, blankets, tents.*

RACHEL, ASHER *and* REBECCA *enter. They are carrying their belongings. They are exhausted.* RACHEL *and* ASHER *are in a state of disbelief.* REBECCA *is calmer. They float across the Square. It all seems a dream, an hallucination. The sounds and colours and people blend into one.*

SINGER: "Meliselda
    Come . . .
    Come to me
    Meliselda . . . "

HAWKER: Paintings of the Messiah. Four hundred reals only. Just a few left. Paintings of the Messiah . . .

HAWKER: The sayings of Sabbatai. Six hundred reals for one scroll. The sayings of our Lord, Sabbatai Sevi . . .

SINGER: "Meliselda
    Come . . .
    Come to me
    Meliselda . . .
    Daughter of my king
    Come to my bed
    I'll touch your ruby lips
    Come to my bed
    Meliselda
    Come . . ."

VISIONARY: And Sabbatai raised his right hand and, lo, the walls of the temple sprang from the earth, and with his left hand, he summoned forth the armies of Israel, the Lost Tribes sailing in snow-white vessels toward the sun . . .

HAWKER: Sarah. Portraits of Sarah. The orphan. The wanderer. The Messiah's wife. Sarah. Beautiful. Mysterious. Only twelve reals. A special bargain.

HAWKER: Tents. For your family. Only a few tents left . . .

GUARD: Entrance to the fortress for one thousand reals . . . we guarantee a glimpse of the Messiah . . .

VISIONARY: And Sabbatai will enter Jerusalem on a celestial lion, guarded by a serpent with seven heads . . .

SINGER: "Meliselda
Come . . .
Come to me
Meliselda . . ."

> [*The* HAWKERS *importune* ASHER. *He looks at them but seems not to see. Eventually, he focusses on the* HAWKER *selling tents. He counts his money. He refuses a tent, but takes some of his money and buys a large blanket. Then, thoroughly laden down, he continues to walk with* RACHEL *and* REBECCA, *still dazed across the square.*]

VOICES: Sabbatai . . .
Sabbatai . . .
Sabbatai . . .
Meliselda . . .

> [*Blackout.*]

Lights rise on RACHEL *praying. She is still in a state of shock. She looks up at God. She opens her mouth. But she cannot speak.*

> [*Blackout.*]

Lights rise on RACHEL *praying. She still cannot speak. She shakes
her head.*

RACHEL: Oh, my God.
      [*Blackout.*]

Lights rise on RACHEL *praying. She has regained some composure.*

RACHEL: So this is land. Dear God, why do you always make
yesterday seem better? When I'm on the boat, I want
land. When I touch the ground, I want the waves.
What's wrong with me? [*Pause.*] Did you ever see so
many people? Of course. *You* have. Crossing the Red
Sea, leaving Egypt, all of that. But we don't get this kind
of thing in Yultishk. [*Pause.*] Oh, Yultishk. [*Pause.*] Do
you know where we are? A hill. I want to be in a house.
No, Asher found a hill, so we can see Sabbatai when he
passes. But when is he going to pass? When is he going to
leave that prison? When is he getting our land back from
the Sultan, and the crown of Judea? Suppose he decides
to wait until Spring. I can't spend winter on a hill.
[*Pause.*] Asher put up a blanket. To protect Mama and
me from the wind, when we sleep. Asher sleeps outside
the blanket, of course. Of course. So I don't have impure
thoughts. [*Pause.*] What am I doing on this hill with this
boy? [*Pause.*] Dear God, help me think *only* of Sabbatai.
Sabbatai . . . [*Pause.*] Sabbatai.
      [*Blackout.*]

*Lights rise on a hillside. Rocks, leading down to a square. The
large Oriental blanket is hanging, attached to the ground with
rope and pegs. There is a slight wind blowing.* REBECCA *sits to the
side, on the ground. A black shawl is draped around her shoulders.
She still carries her wool. She seems to be waiting. Or, at least,
listening to the wind.* RACHEL *and* ASHER *are seated on the ground*

in front of the blanket. They are reading pamphlets. There are pamphlets everywhere. ASHER is in some kind of fervour.

RACHEL: Sabbatai . . . Sabbatai says this . . . Sabbatai says that . . . I can't keep up . . .

ASHER: [*Shows her a pamphlet.*] Look. When the Messiah comes, everything changes. [*He points to a passage.*] See. It says so in the Zohar. There's a whole new system. All the old concepts of right and wrong are swept away. The ritual code is no longer binding. *Everything* changes. [*He gives her another pamphlet.*] See. Here. He's made new feast days. He's made a new Sabbath. He sings new psalms. He sings the song of Meliselda in the synagogue. As an allegory for the Messiah sleeping with the daughter of a king. The Torah. The daughter of God.

RACHEL: The Messiah sleeps with his wife.

ASHER: The Torah.

RACHEL: No. Sarah.

ASHER: Well — they're different kinds of wives.

RACHEL: Do you know what they say about her?

ASHER: I don't listen to gossip. [*He opens another pamphlet.*] Look at this . . .

RACHEL: They say she's a sorceress. They say she's known Satan. *Worse.* They say she's a Catholic. How could the Messiah marry a Catholic? They say she sleeps with many men. She wanders through the tents at night . . .

ASHER: *This*! [*He shakes the pamphlet at her.*] This is what you should think about. Not idle fantasies. And in the synagogue — look! [*He points to a sentence.*] In the synagogue, *everyone* can pronounce the forbidden name of God.

RACHEL: But it's forbidden.

ASHER: No longer. Nothing is forbidden. The Messiah is here. Once there's redemption, then everything is without sin.

Then there is no sin. We're free. There is no more
spiritual oppression. Do you understand that? It's a new
world. We're free!

RACHEL: You're not going to faint again, are you?

ASHER: [*embarrassed*] No.

RACHEL: The last time you fainted you bumped your head.

ASHER: Don't make fun of me. Here. Look. I have something
to show you.

> [ASHER *takes out a small bag and removes a piece of
> meat.*]

RACHEL: What is it?

ASHER: Animal fat.

RACHEL: What?

ASHER: A kidney. With fat. It's all right. It's cooked. I bought
it in the square. Sabbatai says we can eat it.

RACHEL: It's not kosher.

ASHER: Sabbatai said we can eat it.

RACHEL: It says in the Talmud, your soul will be cut off if you
eat animal fat . . .

ASHER: Sabbatai said we can eat it.

RACHEL: It says in the Talmud it's as bad as incest.

ASHER: Sabbatai said we can eat it. Here. See. [*He hands her
another pamphlet.*] It says so.

RACHEL: [*Reads the pamphlet.*] Yes. It does say so. [*Pause.*] What
are you going to do?

ASHER: I'm going to eat it.

> [*Pause.*]

RACHEL: Oh. [*Pause.*] It doesn't look very good.

> [*They both look at the meat. Silence.*]

ASHER: Sabbatai says . . .

RACHEL: Well, if he says . . .

> [*Silence.* ASHER *takes out a knife and cuts the meat in
> two.*]

ASHER: Here.

[*He hands* RACHEL *a piece of meat.*]

RACHEL: What's this?

ASHER: For you.

RACHEL: I don't want it.

ASHER: It's for *you*.

RACHEL: No.

ASHER: Come on . . .

RACHEL: Take it back.

ASHER: It's for you!

RACHEL: I said I don't want it.

> [*She returns the meat to him.*]

ASHER: You have to, Tanta.

RACHEL: Don't call me Tanta. [*She takes her piece back from him.*]
All right. I'm not *that* much older than you. Don't call me
Tanta.

> [*A long pause.*]

Well?

ASHER: You first.

RACHEL: Me?

ASHER: Yes.

RACHEL: No. *You*

ASHER: The woman is always first.

RACHEL: Since when?

> [*Silence. They stare at the meat.*]

Are you afraid? [*Pause.*] What's this I see? I don't believe
it. A *doubt*?

ASHER: No. [*He looks at the meat.*] Never. [*He grabs the meat and
holds it up.*] Never. There's a benediction. Sabbatai has a
benediction. "Blessed are thou, oh Lord, our God, who
has permitted the forbidden." [*He closes his eyes and pops
the meat into his mouth. He chews.*] There. [*He swallows.*] I
did it. [*Jumps about.*] I did it! See! Lightning didn't strike.
Sabbatai *knows*. [*Pause.*] Well?

RACHEL: You still have a little piece left.

ASHER: It's your turn.
         [*Pause.*]
RACHEL: All right. Yes. Sabbatai knows. [*Pause.*] All right.
    [*Pause.*] "Blessed are thou, oh Lord, our God, who has
    permitted the forbidden." [*She stares at the meat.*] I can't.
ASHER: You must.
RACHEL: I'm afraid.
ASHER: Don't you want a new world? Don't you? [*Pause.*]
    Rachel?
         [RACHEL *stares at him.*]
RACHEL: Oh yes.
         [*She puts the meat into her mouth. She pauses. She eats it.
         Silence.*]
ASHER: Well?
         [*Silence.*]
RACHEL: Well. I suppose then . . . it's a new world.
         [*Blackout.*]

Lights rise on RACHEL *praying.*

RACHEL: Well Lord, now there are *your* laws and *his* laws.
    [*Pause.*] And they're day and night. But *he* represents *you*.
    [*Pause.*] Doesn't he? [*Pause.*] So why are there his laws
    and your laws? [*Pause.*] I'm confused. [*Pause.*] I'll bet
    you're confused too. For once. [*Pause.*] Who do I pray to?
    Him? Or you? Both? Do I tell him some things — and
    you others? [*Pause.*] I think I'd rather talk to *him* about
    my teeth. He might sympathize. And my impure
    thoughts. [*Pause.*] He'd say they were pure. [*Pause.*] Day
    and night. [*Pause.*] Listen — I think the two of you have
    to get together and sort things out. [*Pause.*] You know,
    tomorrow is Tisha be'Ab. A very solemn holiday. The
    anniversary of the demolition of the second temple. Well
    — it is also *his* birthday. And he has *abolished* Tisha

be'Ab. He's made it into a feast day. What do you think
of *that*! [*Pause.*] He certainly has a lot more spice than
Jesus, doesn't he? Oh God. He'll probably be just like
Jesus. He'll die a martyr, and someone will start a whole
new religion, and then they'll all go out and kill a lot of
Jews. [*Pause.*] No. It's different. He *is* the Messiah.
[*Pause.*] I know you. You're up to something aren't you?
I can feel it. You're up to something.

    [*Blackout.*]

Lights rise on the hillside. There is a full moon. Music and shouting
— far away — in the square. RACHEL *is sitting with* REBECCA.

RACHEL: Look at the moon. Mama? Look.

    [REBECCA *looks up, then away.*]

There's a breeze. [*Silence.*] Asher's down there. Can you
hear the singing? They all sound drunk. They must be
dancing too. It's Sabbatai's birthday. [*Silence.*] He didn't
ask me to go. Well, I don't like dancing.

    [RACHEL *gets up and wanders over to a rock. She sits*
    down. She looks up at the moon. She hears a young man
    and woman laughing — off — in the rocks. She rises,
    busies herself, clears away some debris in front of the
    blanket, then walks behind the blanket. Silence. A
    WOMAN *enters. She is startlingly beautiful. The woman,*
    SARAH, *is surrounded by a group of* MEN *and* WOMEN
    paying her court. They are laughing. One of them is play-
    ing a mandolin. Another is carrying a jug of wine. Some
    of them have wine goblets. SARAH *is restless. She pays no*
    attention to her companions. She looks at the hillside and
    notices the moon. She sits on a rock. The MANDOLIN
    PLAYER *sits at her feet and continues his melody. Someone*
    hands SARAH *a wine goblet. She drinks. She looks around.*
    She sees REBECCA *on the other side of the hill.* SARAH

rises, as if drawn by a magnet. She walks to REBECCA. REBECCA *turns and looks at her.* SARAH *shudders, but does not take her eyes off* REBECCA.]

SARAH: I know. I can see it in your eyes. [*Pause.*] I know who you talk to. [*She turns to her friends.*] Leave us alone.

[*Her* COMPANIONS *start down the rocks. The* MANDOLIN PLAYER *brings* SARAH *some wine. She takes the jug and his goblet. He rejoins the others as they leave.*]

Is he here now? [*She pours wine into the goblet.*] There's only one who you talk to. Isn't there? [*She smiles.*] Of course. [*She hands* REBECCA *the goblet.*] Here.

[REBECCA *looks at* SARAH. *She takes the goblet and drinks.*]

I can feel him. We used to know each other. No longer. I don't dare to talk to him now. Not in my position.

[SARAH *takes the goblet from* REBECCA. *She drinks. She sits next to* REBECCA.]

Do you know what he did today, my Sabbatai? He composed a new psalm. It's pretty. He likes music. He's in a good mood. He's a creature of moods. Sometimes they're happy — exalted — and his eyes blaze with the magic of a Messiah. Sometimes they're low and melancholy and he mumbles and sleeps. My Sabbatai. Here. Have some more.

[*She hands the goblet to* REBECCA *and pours more wine into it.*]

I mixed it myself. From five different wines. Gifts. Look at the moon.

[*She rises and looks at the sky.* REBECCA *slowly drinks from the goblet.*]

Is that where he is? Behind the moon? When do you talk to him? [*She looks at* REBECCA.] I can see everything in your eyes. I know everything.

[*She takes the goblet from* REBECCA *and drinks. She sits.*]

There was a moon in the cemetery. When they found me.
You must know the story. Everyone knows the story.
They all tell the story. When they found me. I escaped
from the convent. They carried me off to the convent
when the Cossacks came. Oh, yes, the Cossacks. I see it
in your eyes. They made me become a Catholic. That's
when I started to talk to him. In the convent. The nuns
knew him. Oh, yes. One night my father came to me in a
dream. He was still bleeding. The Cossack knife. My
dead father. He said, "You are a Jewess." I fled the
convent. They found me in a cemetery. A rabbi and his
wife. And I said, "I am Sarah. I am a Jewess. I shall
marry the Messiah." Drink some more.

> [*She fills the goblet and hands it to* REBECCA. REBECCA
> *drinks.*]

The wines come from Amsterdam, Venice, Leghorn,
Hamburg and Alexandria. I know each city. I travelled
for years, looking for the Messiah. When I found him, he
was in Cairo. He married me at once. You know they say
Sabbatai is handsome. He's not. He's rather plain. They
tell stories about my travels. About men. Men and mad-
ness. Well. They don't understand convents. I didn't
speak to him again, after that — the convent. And, of
course, now I can't. [*Silence.*] But somebody must. I
know you. You have the eyes of my father. I know what
you've seen. Those things must never happen again. Life
has to change. We have suffered enough. We need a
Messiah. [*Pause.*] Of course I always thought the Messiah
would be golden. Riding a chariot, riding a lion, riding a
dragon. I thought he would be a pillar of fire with eyes
and a mouth. Not a rather plain man who gets depressed.
And has stomach aches. But he's the only Messiah we
have. I know. I walked across Poland, I walked across
Europe, I walked across the Holy Land. Searching. He

composed a psalm today, my Sabbatai. Sweet Sabbatai.

> [*She takes* REBECCA*'s hand.*]

The one you talk to. Tell him to leave us alone. Tell him
to stay behind the moon. Tell him I said so. He remembers
me. I am Sarah. A Jewess. Bride of the Messiah.

> [*She kisses* REBECCA.]

Please.

> [SARAH *pours some more wine.* RACHEL *comes out from
> behind the blanket. She is startled to see someone with her
> mother. She walks to* SARAH *and* REBECCA. *She recognizes*
> SARAH.]

RACHEL: Are you . . . ?

> [*She falls to her knees in front of* SARAH. SARAH *draws*
> RACHEL *up.* SARAH *looks at* REBECCA, *then at* RACHEL.]

SARAH: Oh, yes.

> [SARAH *takes her hands and places them over* RACHEL*'s
> face. She moves her hands down to* RACHEL*'s mouth.*
> SARAH *closes her eyes. She presses a healing warmth into*
> RACHEL*'s mouth.*]

Don't be afraid.

> [SARAH *pulls her hands away. She looks back at* REBECCA,
> then turns and walks to the other side of the hill. She sits
> on a rock and watches the moon.* RACHEL *sits next to her
> mother.* REBECCA *hands* RACHEL *the goblet.* RACHEL *is
> surprised at her mother's gesture.* REBECCA *looks at*
> RACHEL. RACHEL *drinks the wine.* REBECCA *puts her
> arms around* RACHEL. RACHEL *leans back against her
> mother.* REBECCA *strokes her.* RACHEL *weeps. A mandolin.*
> SARAH*'s* COMPANIONS *return. She rises and starts off
> with them. She turns and looks back at* REBECCA. *She
> leaves with her friends. The* MANDOLIN PLAYER *lingers a
> moment, playing a tune against the moon.* ASHER *enters.
> He is drunk. He sits next to the* MANDOLIN PLAYER. *He
> hums the tune.* RACHEL *sees* ASHER. *She rises. She walks*

towards him. The MANDOLIN PLAYER *starts down the rocks. His melody can be heard for a long time trailing off in the distance.* ASHER *rises. He is unsteady.* RACHEL *walks up to him. She stares at him. A long silence.*]

RACHEL: "Blessed are thou, oh Lord, our God, who has permitted that which is forbidden."

[RACHEL *unbuttons her blouse. She takes* ASHER*'s face in her hands. She kisses him, passionately. Her hand explores his body. She continues to kiss him. Then she pulls away. She stares at him.* ASHER *is silent. She continues to stare at him.* ASHER *bends and kisses her breasts. His lips move up her body. They stop. Then he kisses her mouth.*]

ASHER: Tanta, Tanta . . .

[*The sound of the mandolin has almost disappeared.* RACHEL *and* ASHER *embrace and move behind the curtain. Silence.* REBECCA *sits staring at the moon. A wolf howls. A shadow crosses the moon. The night is darker.* REBECCA *rises. She walks to the centre of the hillside. She takes her roll of wool and unravels it. She spreads the wool out on the ground. In a large circle. She stands in the centre of the circle.*]

REBECCA: Where are you?

[*There is a long silence. The night gets darker. The wings of a bat can be heard flapping against a rock.* REBECCA *stares out into the night.*]

I remember you. I remember you. You came for my husband and my child. You rode into town with the Cossacks. You ripped my baby from my arms. You tore my baby to bits: like a piece of meat. You roasted the pieces. You took my husband . . . Oh yes, I remember you. You pointed to my husband and said to the Cossacks, that's him, that's the man who collects the taxes. I saw your face. I heard your voice. It was you who hired him.

I remember you. You took my husband . . . I held my
daughter. People were screaming. People were burning.
I ran. I remember you. I looked behind me. I could still
see my husband. I wandered. We all did. We had no
homes. I had my daughter. She was young. Her face
turned ugly. She saw too much. She forgot what she saw.
Her face remembered. We reached a town. The Cossacks
came again. We ran. I saw you — always — racing with
them. I remember you. You took my husband. Everyone
was fighting. You got bored. The Cossacks were gone. I
went home. I hated my home. I saw your face. I heard
your voice. At night I called out to you. They thought I
was silent. I was calling to you. You took my husband.
He was alive. That's the man who collects the taxes, you
said. They took a cat. You gave them a cat. They sewed
the cat up in my husband's belly. He was alive. They
fastened him to a beam. The cat in his belly. Oh yes. I
saw you. I called your name at night. They thought I
was silent. They didn't want to hear your name. They
talked to God. I talked to you. They thought I was silent.
I was never silent.

　　　[*Pause. She paces around in a circle. She stops.*]
And now where are you? Behind the moon? No. You've
always been much closer than that. Are you waiting for
your moment? Are you ready to return? No! The Messiah
is here! Leave him be. Stay away. He doesn't want to see
you. He doesn't want to hear you. The Messiah is here!
You're starting to fade. Leave him be. I can't remember
your face. I can't remember your voice. Oh my beloved.
My dearest, my beautiful demon of the night. Fade
away. Fade away. We are saved!

　　　[*Blackout.*]

Lights rise on the hillside. Morning. REBECCA *is asleep against a rock. The woollen circle remains.* RACHEL *emerges from behind the blanket. She looks up at the sky. She is about to pray. She stops herself. She smiles. She sees the wool. She gathers it up, returns it in a pile to her mother and lays it at her feet.* ASHER *comes out from behind the blanket.* RACHEL *goes to him. They embrace.* RACHEL *and* ASHER *lie in front of the blanket, looking at the sky.* ASHER *begins to sing.*

ASHER: "Meliselda
　　Come . . .
　　Come to me
　　Meliselda . . . "
　　　　[*Blackout.*]

Lights rise on RACHEL *praying.*

RACHEL: God bless Asher. [*She smiles.*] Yes I know. I haven't talked to you for days. For days and days and days . . . [*She laughs.*] I start to. All the time. Then my mind drifts. Drifts . . . [*Pause.*] I'm happy. I suppose people don't pray as much when they're happy, do they? Well, you see, if you just made people happier, you'd get some rest. [*She smiles.*] Oh Lord, I love it. I love making love. I was right, Reb Ellis, that had nothing to do with making love. I'm in love with Asher making love. [*Pause.*] I don't love him as much when he talks. It's always the same thing. Sabbatai, Sabbatai. Now Reb Ellis talked in circles, but circles have some kind of dimension. I liked that. Oh, this is why I didn't want to speak to you. It's going to get confusing again. It's not going to be simple. [*Pause.*] Yes. It is. It *is* simple. [*Pause.*] Do you know what Asher said the other night? He said I was beautiful. And this is what's amazing. I accepted it. I didn't argue. I didn't blush. I said "Thank

you. I know." [*Pause.*] As if I always knew. [*Pause.*] He
said, "You're beautiful, Tanta!" [*Pause.*] Ah. Tanta.
[*Pause.*] Now. *This* is the problem. I'm not beautiful
because I'm beautiful. After all, I'm *not* beautiful. I'm
beautiful because I'm forbidden. Or was once. Do you
know what I mean? Not only is he, an unmarried man,
an unmarried *boy* for that matter, having sexual inter-
course — but with his aunt as well. It's vague incest. Not
the real thing. I'm not even an aunt by blood. Still. It
counts. And I suppose I didn't help things that first
night by tearing off my clothes and throwing 'forbidden'
in his face. Oh God. I must have been mad. I must have
been drunk. [*She smiles.*] I enjoyed it. [*Pause.*] Still.
Tanta. Sabbatai says he should explore the forbidden.
Bad is good. [*Pause.*] Ugly is beautiful. [*Silence.*] I don't
know if I understand Sabbatai's logic. But I never understood the Kabbalah. The parts I've heard about. Still.
[*Pause.*] It isn't me, is it? It's Sabbatai. [*Pause.*] Asher is
sleeping with Sabbatai. [*Pause.*] Oh Lord, you know
what the Bible misses? And the Talmud? And all the
rabbis? And probably the Kabbalah as well? [*Pause.*]
Your exquisite sense of humour.

> [*Blackout.*]

Lights rise on the hillside. REBECCA *sits at the side, looking
straight ahead.* RACHEL *is again lying in* ASHER's *arms.* ASHER *is
singing.*

ASHER: "Meliselda
    Come . . .
    Come to me
    Meliselda . . ."
RACHEL: Don't you know any other songs?
ASHER: It's Sabbatai's.

RACHEL: I know. [*Pause.*] Asher?

ASHER: What?

RACHEL: When is the day of redemption coming? When is
    Sabbatai going to take his crown? When do we follow
    him to Jerusalem?

ASHER: When he says so.

RACHEL: Isn't it taking a long time?

ASHER: Why do you always ask so many questions?

RACHEL: Don't you ever wonder? Just a little? Why is Sabbatai
    in a prison? It *is* a prison, Asher. He holds court like a
    king, but it *is* a prison. Dignitaries visit him from all over
    the world. But it is a prison. Don't you ever wonder?
    Why doesn't he knock the walls down? And leave?

ASHER: He has reasons for everything. It's not for us to under-
    stand. You mustn't question him.

RACHEL: You're a child.

ASHER: What?

RACHEL: A child. A child. [*Pause. She kisses him.*] A child.
        [REBECCA *suddenly springs up. She moves to the front of
        the hillside, listening.*]
    Mama, what is it?
        [*In the distance, a hum. It grows louder. People can be
        heard shouting.* RACHEL *and* ASHER *move to opposite
        sides of the hill, overlooking the edge.* REBECCA *stands in
        the centre, also at the edge, looking down. The shouting
        grows louder.* RACHEL *and* ASHER *call to each other across
        the hill.*]

ASHER: Can you see anything?

RACHEL: The sun's in my eyes.

ASHER: Look . . .

RACHEL: Where?

ASHER: A procession.

RACHEL: Where?

ASHER: Can't you see?

RACHEL: A little. Turks.

ASHER: Listen! His name! They're calling his name!

RACHEL: [*startled*] Sabbatai.

ASHER: It must be him.

> [ASHER *runs back to the blanket, completely excited and
> disorientated. He looks for something.*]

RACHEL: I see something.

ASHER: What?

RACHEL: A horse. I think it's a horse.

ASHER: Where are my things? I have to go down there.
Where's my shirt?

> [RACHEL *turns to help him.*]

No. Keep looking. Tell me what you see.

RACHEL: Nothing. People. A blur. The wind's blowing. A
horse. Yes. Definitely. A horse.

ASHER: He's left the prison. He's going to the Sultan. [*He finds
his shirt.*] You see. You ask questions. You have no faith.
He left the prison. When he wanted to. Where are my
shoes?

> [RACHEL *turns to him.*]

RACHEL: You're in a state.

ASHER: What do you see?

RACHEL: [*turning back*] Nothing. Just a horse.

ASHER: Is that all? A horse? That's all you see?

RACHEL: Yes. No. I think . . . Someone's on the horse.

ASHER: It's him! My shoes!

RACHEL: I can make out an arm . . .

ASHER: He's going that way. [*He points in the direction of the
noise.*] And that way is Constantinople.

RACHEL: They're blocking my view. I only see an arm.

ASHER: He's going to Constantinople.

RACHEL: It's waving. The arm is waving!

ASHER: [*now fully dressed*] He's claiming the crown. He's taking
us back to Jerusalem. I've got to follow him.

[ASHER, *in a frenzy, runs down the side of the hill.* RACHEL *does not see him disappear. The noise begins to fade off into the distance.*]

RACHEL: I saw his arm. Sabbatai's arm. I think. I'm not sure. I guess. It's passed. Asher . . .

[*She turns and sees that* ASHER *is gone.*]

Asher!

[*Blackout.*]

Lights rise on RACHEL *praying, almost trance-like.*

RACHEL: God bless Sabbatai. God bless Mama. God bless Asher. God bless Tanta Rose. God bless the soul of Reb Ellis. God bless Papa. Papa's soul. Thank you. Thank you for bringing the Messiah. Forgive me for ever doubting him. Forgive me for asking so many questions. God bless Sabbatai. Don't let the Sultan harm him. God bless Sabbatai. Don't let the Turks touch him. Thank you. Thank you for leading him out of the fortress, into the light, into our dreams. Our dreams of Jerusalem. Thank you. God bless Sabbatai. God bless Sabbatai. God bless the Messiah.

[*Blackout.*]

Lights rise on the hillside. Early morning. RACHEL *and* REBECCA *are sitting, huddled together. It is cold.*

RACHEL: Did you hear something? I thought I heard something. A cry. In the distance. I wish Asher would return. It's getting cold.

[REBECCA *springs up and walks to the edge of the hill.* RACHEL *goes to her.*]

What is it? It's all right, Mama. It's all right. Come on. Sit down. We have to rest. We have a long walk ahead of us.

[RACHEL *leads* REBECCA *back. They sit.*]

I wish we could close our eyes on the hillside and then open them — and be in Jerusalem. Perhaps Sabbatai will do that. But the rest of us are going to have to walk. I know that. [*Pause.*] I wish Asher would return.

[REBECCA *springs up again.*]

Mama!

[RACHEL *goes to the edge of the hillside and stands with* REBECCA. *They listen.*]

Yes. I did hear something. A cry. Someone's crying. Far away.

[ASHER *enters. He is exhausted. And very still. His eyes are glazed. He looks at* RACHEL *and* REBECCA *but doesn't speak. He sits on a rock.* RACHEL *starts towards him.*]

Asher . . .

[REBECCA *stares at* ASHER. *Then — suddenly — she cries out. Then she turns away.*]

What happened?

[ASHER *is silent.*]

Asher.

[RACHEL *touches his shoulder. He pushes her hand aside.*]

We've been waiting for news. For days. Tell us what happened.

[ASHER *is silent.* REBECCA *sits, uttering low, rhythmic moans.* RACHEL *looks at* ASHER, *then at* REBECCA, *then back at* ASHER.]

Now I have *two* people who won't talk. [*Silence.*] I will go mad if you don't tell me what happened.

[ASHER *looks up at her.*]

ASHER: Mehemid Effendi.

RACHEL: What?

ASHER: Aziz Mehemid Effendi.

RACHEL: Who's that?

ASHER: The Keeper of the Palace Gates.

RACHEL: What are you talking about?

ASHER: I'm going to sleep.

RACHEL: You can't. Tell us what happened.

ASHER: I have to sleep.

RACHEL: What happened to Sabbatai?

ASHER: It's not important.

RACHEL: Asher, what's wrong?

ASHER: Nothing's wrong. I'm tired.

RACHEL: Did Sabbatai get the crown?

ASHER: He got something better.

RACHEL: Are we leaving for Jerusalem?

ASHER: It's not important.

RACHEL: Asher. Tell us.

[*She touches his face. He pulls her hand away.*]

ASHER: I'm so tired. All I want to do is sleep. I walked all the way to Adrianople. That's where he went. Not Constantinople. The Sultan's court is in Adrianople. We were all telling each other the name of the wrong city. Isn't that funny? The Sultan's court is in Adrianople. We had everything mixed up. He was to go to Adrianople — not Constantinople — to get his crown.

RACHEL: Did he get the crown?

ASHER: He got something better. I want to go to sleep.

[RACHEL *touches him again.*]

Please. Don't put your hand on me. Please. They took him to the Sultan. The Sultan said: I hear you are the Jewish Messiah. Well, then, I've decided to lead you through the streets of Constantinople — or perhaps he said Adrianople, I don't know which — with flaming torches tied to your body until you slowly burn to death. Of course, if you *are* the Messiah, a miracle will happen. And you will not burn. Better still, make us a miracle right now. Prove to us right now that you are the Messiah.

How can I, said the Messiah. Every day I wait for a sign
from God to prove it to *me*. Well, then, said the Sultan,
you will die.

> [*Pause.*]

RACHEL: He's dead. Sabbatai is dead?

ASHER: Well. There is one other choice, said the Sultan.
Rather than die, you can adopt our religion. No. Sabbatai
is not dead. Sabbatai is a Muslim. Sabbatai threw off his
black hat. Sabbatai embraced Islam. Sabbatai went in for
a crown and emerged with something better — a turban.
The Messiah is not dead. The Messiah is now called
Aziz Mehemid Effendi. The Messiah was given an
honorary office. The Messiah was appointed Keeper of
the Palace Gates. The Messiah will receive a royal pension.
The Messiah is not dead. Jerusalem lives in Adrianople.
Jerusalem lives in the Sultan's palace.

> [RACHEL *gasps. She puts her arms around* ASHER.]

Don't touch me, harlot!

> [*He pushes* RACHEL *away.*]

You made me sin. I ate the fat of a kidney. I danced on
Tisha be'Ab. I slept with my uncle's wife. I waited all my
life for the Messiah. I had no family. I studied the
Kabbalah. I waited. I waited for Aziz Mehemid Effendi!
Keeper of the Palace Gates!

> [ASHER *starts to weep and beat his breast. He tears his*
> *clothes.* RACHEL *moves towards him.*]

RACHEL: Asher, don't . . .

> [*He takes out a knife and aims it at her.*]

ASHER: If you touch me, woman, I will kill you. I want to
sleep. I have to sleep.

> [*He goes behind the blanket. Silence.* RACHEL *stands*
> *dazed. Then she starts to laugh. She cannot stop laughing.*]

> [*Blackout.*]

Lights rise on RACHEL *praying.*

RACHEL: You don't exist. I thought you should know that.
You don't exist. I won't try to find excuses for you.
They're finding them already for Sabbatai. They're
crowding back into the square. Most are cursing him. But
some have excuses. It's all part of a great design. Sabbatai
is disguising himself. Every Messiah is misjudged. God
has his reasons. [*Pause.*] There's no great design. There
are no reasons. There is no God. You don't exist. [*Pause.*]
Poor Sabbatai. Who can blame him? Burning torches?
Feh! This way he gets a pension. Better this than dying
like Jesus. Jesus didn't do us any favours. Dying for you.
There is no you. [*Pause.*] Poor Sabbatai. Well. He was
just a man. That's all. Just a man. Who had even heard
of him a year ago? Not like you. Everyone's *always* heard
of you. You who aren't. You who don't. You who never
were. [*Pause.*] Poor Mehemid Effendi. He was waiting
for a sign. Everybody must be waiting for a sign, then.
Not just me. Well — no longer me. I've got the sign. I've
received the message. I've seen the rainbow. It starts
nowhere and leads nowhere. I've talked to you every day
of my life. I've been talking into thin air. Into space. I've
been trusting space. I've been loving space. Well — no
longer. I can get along without thin air. I don't need anything to believe in. I know that *I* exist. That's enough. So
goodbye.
    [*Blackout.*]

Lights rise on the hillside. Morning. RACHEL *is asleep in front of
the blanket.* REBECCA *is standing in the morning light. She has a
few possessions with her. She is holding her ball of wool. She takes
the wool and unravels it. She makes a circle of wool on the ground
around* RACHEL. *She enters the circle. She kneels down beside*

RACHEL. *She holds her hand on* RACHEL*'s forehead. She kisses*
RACHEL*'s forehead. She rises. She looks straight ahead. She walks*
outside the circle. She takes her long black shawl and wraps it
around her body — and around her face, until only her eyes show.
She stands on the edge of the hillside.

REBECCA: Sabbatai!

> [*She slowly walks down the hillside and disappears. A*
> *long silence. It grows lighter.* RACHEL *wakes up. She sees*
> *the woollen circle. She rises. She looks for* REBECCA. *She*
> *searches the hillside. She stops. She sits on a rock.*]

RACHEL: Oh, Mama.

> [*She rises. She looks at the blanket. She walks to the*
> *blanket.*]

RACHEL: Asher. Come on out. You've slept almost twenty-
four hours. It's enough. You're a child. It's time to grow
up. Asher!

> [*She starts to gather the wool.*]

We didn't do anything wrong. Well — perhaps the kidney
fat. It tasted terrible. But it wasn't wrong to sleep
together. Unless it was wrong for you because you don't
think I'm pretty. But that has nothing to do with the
Messiah. Or laws. That's just *judgement*. It's no sin.
Sabbatai wasn't wrong about everything. Sabbatai did
some good.

> [*She has gathered all the wool. She looks at the blanket.*]

Asher, the Messiah *has* come. He's inside of us. We can
save ourselves. Asher. I *am* beautiful.

> [*She touches the blanket.*]

Come on. You're not a child anymore. You've been
asleep for too long.

> [*She pulls the blanket. It turns itself around.* ASHER *is*
> *clutched against the other side of the blanket, holding his*
> *knife in his stomach. He is dead. Silence.* RACHEL *stumbles*

back. She looks up at the sky. She screams.]

God damn you, God!

[*She throws the wool away.*]

He's a child! He doesn't know the difference! How can you be so cruel?

[*She runs away from the blanket. She paces in circles. She looks up.*]

Why am I talking to you? Stay away from me! You're not there! I hate you! You don't exist! Stay away!

[*She runs in circles, trying to be left alone. Finally she stops.*]

Why am I talking to you!

[*She sits on a rock.*]

[*She looks around her.*]

[*She rises.*]

[*She gathers her belongings and ties them together, using the wool as string.*]

[*She pulls* ASHER*'s body off the blanket and takes the blanket.*]

[*She ties the blanket around her other belongings.*]

[*She starts to move away.*]

[*She stops.*]

[*She returns to* ASHER*'s body.*]

[*She pulls the knife out of his stomach.*]

[*She puts the knife in her pocket.*]

[*She wraps her shawl around her shoulders.*]

[*She holds her belongings. She looks at the hillside.*]

[*She starts to leave.*]

[*She stops.*]

[*She is still.*]

[*She looks up at the sky.*]

I don't want to leave without you. But I don't want you to come with me. I don't know.

[*She starts to leave.*]
[*She stops.*]
I don't know. I don't know.
[*She starts to leave.*]
[*She stops.*]
Oh God. After all of this. I still don't know.
[*She leaves.*]

CURTAIN

Afterpiece

In the early 17th Century there was a vast Jewish population in Poland. Over three hundred thousand strong, it had become an independent, flourishing and self-governing community. Rabbinic civilization was at its height.

Poland itself led a feudal existence. The Jewish community acted as the only buffer between the wealthy noblemen and the impoverished serfs. Deprived by law of most other means of earning a livelihood, the Jews were employed as the visible representatives of the usually absent nobility. They acted as stewards, administered the land, ran the fairs, collected the taxes. They were virtually the only merchants.

The Ukraine was the southeastern borderland. The Ukrainians considered themselves Russian and hated their Polish conquerors. Some Ukrainian peasants formed themselves into marauding and blood-thirsty cavalry squads. They were known as Cossacks.

In 1648 a Cossack chief named Chmielnicki led an uprising against the Poles. After ten years of brutal fighting, peace was restored. Over one third of the Jewish population had been slaughtered, the rest impoverished.

The ravished Jewish community became obsessed with the visions of salvation. Kabbalah, the mystical interpretation of the scriptures, became a primary force. There was an all-consuming certainty that the Messiah would finally arrive.

In 1626 a son was born to a Jewish family of Spanish origin in Smyrna in Asia Minor. His name was Sabbatai Sevi. He was ordained a Sephardic rabbi at the age of eighteen . . .

Martin Sherman
December, 1982